The Instant Intellectual

The Instant Intellectual

THE QUICK & EASY GUIDE TO
SOUNDING SMART & CULTURED

COMPILED AND ANNOTATED BY

Norah Vincent & Chad Conway

HYPERION

NEW YORK

Library of Congress Cataloging-in-Publication Data

Vincent, Norah.

  The instant intellectual / compiled & annotated by Norah Vincent & Chad Conway—1st ed.

   p. cm.

  ISBN 0-7868-6376-5

  1. English language—Foreign words and phrases—Dictionaries. 2. English language—Eponyms—Dictionaries. 3. English language—Terms and phrases. 4. Vocabulary. I. Conway, Chad. II. Title.

PE1670.V56   1998

423'.1—dc21   97–35322

                    CIP

Designed by Jessica Shatan

FIRST EDITION

10 9 8 7 6 5 4 3 2

For my parents, the most incorrigible pedants I know.
N.V.

For Mark Drendel,
the most incorrigible,
period.
C.C.

Acknowledgments

My most heartfelt thanks to Juliet, Bob, Alexander,
and Edward for knowing me and loving me anyway,
to Eric Simonoff for his unflagging support,
David Cashion for saying yes, and Dee Appleman
for teaching me to read and write.

N.V.

To my parents Gregory and Charlotte; Lisa, Neve,
and Barbara Conway, to whom I owe everything;
to Alex Schnubb, Anthony Belardo, and David Burry;
to Michael Chaban and A. J. Pietrantone, and Jerry
Dalven; to Eric Simonoff and David Cashion,
thank you.

C.C.

Note to the Reader

Do not read this book cover to cover,
in the predictable linear fashion.

Immerse yourself in the milieu you never had.

Soak in the manner of the dilettante
and emerge cultured, urbane, superior.

Or at least sounding so.

Achilles' heel

[uh-kill-ees-heel]

A weak spot.

Achilles was the hero of Homer's epic
poem, the *Iliad*, and represented
the Greek prototype of the beautiful,
courageous, and nearly undefeatable warrior.
As a child, Achilles was dipped
in the river Styx by his mother,
a process that made him invulnerable
except in the spot by which his
mother held him, the heel.

*Lady Macbeth's Achilles' heel was ambition,
and Macbeth's was Lady Macbeth.*

ad hoc

[add-hock]

To this.
A term used most often in politics
or organizations when committees
are formed to deal specifically
with one issue or set of issues.
It has also come to mean slapdash,
off the cuff, thrown together.

*Opponents of psychotherapy
often consider it a rather ad hoc
and bogus science.*

ad hominem

[add-hahm-in-em]

To the man.
When an opponent attacks you personally
instead of attacking your ideas.

*The following joke that circulated
during the 1996 Presidential campaign
was an ad hominem attack:*

*If Bill Clinton's building a bridge
to the next century, let's hope
Ted Kennedy's not driving us across it.*

ad infinitum

[add-in-fin-eye-tum]

To infinity.
Without end or limit.

*The English poet Rupert Brooke will
be remembered ad infinitum as the
picture of gilded youth off
to die in the Great War:*

*"And if I should die
Know that a corner of some foreign field
Will be forever England."*

ad libitum

[add-li-bee-tum]

To desire.
In accordance with desire.
In English we might say, "As you wish,"
though we do often use a shortened
form of this Latin phrase
in common speech:

Any skilled actor will tell you
that when you forget
your lines during a performance,
there's only one thing to do—ad lib,
and quickly.

a priori

[eh-pry-or-eye]

Knowledge you possess prior to,
or without experience.

*You don't have to be a bachelor to know
that all bachelors are unmarried.*

a posteriori

[eh-post-ear-ee-or-eye]

Knowledge gained after or through experience.

*You do have to have been married to know
that you should have stayed a bachelor.*

a fortiori

[eh-for-she-or-eye]

All the more so. Moreover.

Some men might say that alimony and menopause are the best reasons of all to stay a bachelor.

Or, as Mark Twain said, "Experience gives you good judgment and bad judgment gives you experience."

ad nauseam

[add-naw-zee-am]

To nausea.
To a sickening or excessive degree.

*There's nothing more uninspiring than
a minister who drones on ad nauseam about
hellfire and brimstone.*

agent provocateur

[ah-jawn-pro-vock-a-tur]

Secret agent.

*An undercover cop might be considered
an agent provocateur, because he
will incite suspected criminals to some
illegal acts that will make them
liable to punishment.*

agitprop

[a-jit-prop]

Agitation and propaganda.
A portmanteau word, or literal packing
of two words into one.
Generally associated with Communist
and radical left-wing strategies for
gaining power and disseminating
the party line.

*Agitprop was teamster rabble-rouser
Jimmy Hoffa's forte.*

aide-de-camp

[aid-duh-camp]

An assistant, gofer, or sidekick.

Dr. Watson was Sherlock Holmes's aide-de-camp.
Friday was Robinson Crusoe's.
George Stephanopoulos was Bill Clinton's.
Ed McMahon was Johnny Carson's.

alfresco

[al-fresco]

Outdoors. In the open air.

Dining alfresco is most pleasant in the early fall,
when the swelter of summer has passed,
and there is a soupçon of coolness in the air.

alma mater

[ahl-muh-ma-tur]

Fostering mother.
The school you attended;
usually college or university.

Yale is George Bush's alma mater.

Amerika

A distinctly unaffectionate term
for the United States,
probably taken from the title of an
unfinished novel by Franz Kafka.
It deals with the misadventures
of a young European in a very strange and
expressionistically depicted America.
Thus, the "k" lends a certain surreality to
the familiar, as Kafka was wont to do.
It was co-opted in the 1960s by American
radicals, and expressed their belief that
our beloved "free" land was really as corrupt
and authoritarian as any fascist regime.

*Amerika will be the land of the free
only as long as it remains the home of the brave.*

amor fati

[ah-more-fah-tee]

Love of fate.
The stoical acceptance or belief in the
predetermined nature of all things.
Commonly expressed as "que sera sera"
or "what will be will be."

*Calvinists possess amor fati because
they believe in predestination.*

amour-propre

[ah-moor-pro-pruh]

Self-respect.

*In the face of great humiliation, robust amour-propre
will often carry you through, head held high.*

angry young man

A character type who appeared in
the works of a group
of young British writers during the
mid-twentieth century.
He expresses the bitterness of the lower
classes toward the establishment,
and is exemplified best in John Osborne's
1956 play *Look Back in Anger*.

Knowing this will save you from the
embarrassment of referring to JFK Jr.
as an angry young man.
Those born with silver flatware
in orifices need not apply.

anima mundi

[an-i-muh-mun-dee]

The spirit of the world.
Anima, meaning soul or life, and mundi,
meaning world.

*The 1939 World's Fair was an expression
of the anima mundi before World War II.*

Anschluss

[on-shluss]

An alliance, union, pact, or treaty between parties.
Specifically, the pact Germany and Austria made
in 1938 on the eve of World War II.

*The marriage of Harold Evans and
Tina Brown is considered, by some literati,
to be a daunting Anschluss.*

antebellum

[an-tea-bell-um]

Before the war/prewar.

*The title of Margaret Mitchell's famous
and beloved novel was an elegy
to the antebellum South, whose resplendent
beauty and "peculiar institution" were,
by the end of the Civil War,
indeed gone with the wind.*

apparatchik

[ap-are-at-chick]

A Russian party bureaucrat.
A small fry who works for and is loyal
to a political party or apparat.

*Those annoying people who distribute campaign
leaflets in the subway are apparatchiks.*

Apollonian

[ap-oh-lone-ee-an]

Restrained, stoic, disciplined, of or concerned
with what is classically beautiful.
Referring to the Greek god Apollo.

Popularized by Nietzsche in his book
The Birth of Tragedy.

Dionysian

[die-oh-nice-ee-an]

Orgiastic, reckless.
Referring to Dionysus, the Greek God of wine.
The opposite of Apollonian. Characterized by
debauchery; a wild lifestyle concerned mainly
with the pursuit of pleasure.

*Olympic gymnasts, libraries,
and concertos are Apollonian.
Fraternity parties are Dionysian.*

antediluvian

[an-ti-dih-loo-vee-an]

Ante, before, and diluvium, flood. Before the flood.
Prior to the great biblical flood from which Noah
saved the animals. Used to describe a time before a
catastrophe or simply a time long, long ago.

*In the age of laptops, the Macintosh Plus
seems positively antediluvian.*

après moi le déluge

[a-pray-mwa-le-day-looge]

After me the flood.
French proverb, sometimes seen as
"après nous le déluge," or, after us, the flood.

*Famously quipped by the Marquise de Pompadour to
Louis XV after the defeat of the French army by
Frederick the Great in the battle of Rossbach.*

auto-da-fé

[aw-tow-dah-fay]

The event and festival surrounding a burning at
the stake by order of the Spanish Inquisition.
Used to describe any ritual denunciation,
torture, or violent humiliation.

In Leonard Bernstein's musical Candide,
*the bloodthirsty crowds merrily sing
"What a day, what a day for an auto-da-fé."*

avant-garde

[ah-vont-guard]

Front guard. Vanguard. The groundbreaking
forefront of a movement, usually artistic,
musical, or intellectual.

*Greenwich Village, New York City,
has always been home to the avant-garde.*

babushka

[bah-bush-ka]

A head scarf. A Russian grandmother or old
woman who wears such a head scarf.

*In Kiev, it is said that babushkas are allowed
to upbraid publicly anyone who provokes them.
Custom has it that they have earned that right.*

Babushka

belle époque

[bell-e-pawk]

An era of cultural and social refinement.
France at the end of the nineteenth century.

The Renaissance was a belle époque.

belle laide

[bell-led]

It means beautiful and ugly at the same time.
Classically unattractive but infused with beauty.

Sandra Bernhard is a belle laide.

belles-lettres

[bell-let-truh]

Beautiful letters.

Literature that is an end in itself,
not revered for its content or its practical value
but because it is well wrought.

*His writing is a reflection of himself;
indeed belles-lettres, useless,
but beautiful.*

bête noire

[bet-nwar]

Black beast.
Pet peeve.
Bugbear.
Someone or something that you
dislike intensely and avoid.

*Clarence Thomas was Anita Hill's bête noire.
And vice versa.*

beyond the pale

Beyond the limits of good taste.
Overkill.
Gratuitous.

*Pouring salt in a wound is beyond the pale,
as is speaking ill of the dead.*

Bildungsroman

[bill-dungs-ro-mahn]

A coming-of-age novel that follows the progress
of its hero from childhood to adulthood.

A Portrait of the Artist as a Young Man
by James Joyce, and
Of Human Bondage *by W. Somerset Maugham
are both Bildungsromans.*

billet-doux

[bill-ay-doo]

Soft ticket, note or letter.
A love letter.

*What was intended to be an invective became,
in effect, a billet-doux.*

bluestocking

A derisive term for an intellectual,
literary, and usually pedantic woman.
From the Bluestocking Club,
an eighteenth-century literary club
that met at the home of Elizabeth Montagu.
Purportedly, the name is derived from
the sartorial habits of its members,
who wore informal blue stockings
instead of the customary formal white.

*The female members of the
Algonquin Round Table
were bluestockings extraordinaire.*

bona fide

[bone-uh-fied]

Good faith.
Real or genuine.

John Wayne Gacey was a bona fide mass murderer.

bon mot

[bawn-mo]

Good word.
A well-expressed, often witty turn of phrase.

Or, as the inimitable Dorothy Parker
once said of bons mots,
"If, with the literate, I am
compelled to try an epigram,
I never seek to take the credit;
we all assume that Oscar said it."

Boswell

Somebody who becomes known for
writing the definitive biography
of a famous person.
John Boswell was the faithful recorder
of the life and words of the great
eighteenth-century polymath Samuel Johnson.
He wrote *Boswell's Life of Samuel Johnson*, 1791,
and *Journal of the Tour to the Hebrides*, 1785.

*Some would argue that David Herbert Donald
is Abraham Lincoln's Boswell.*

bread and circuses

Food and entertainment.
From the Roman satirist Juvenal who wrote,
"The people that once bestowed commands,
consulships, legions, and all else,
now concerns itself no more, and longs
eagerly for just two things—
bread and circuses!"

*Pizza and football games
are the modern American's
bread and circuses.*

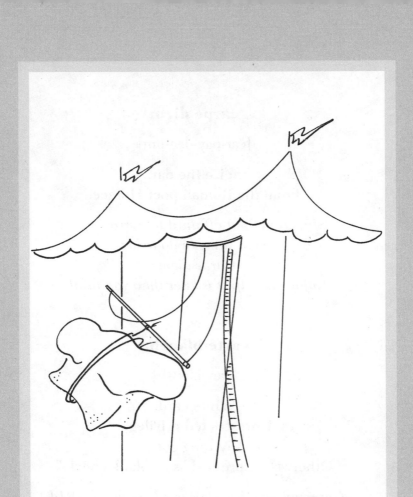

Bread and Circuses

carpe diem

[car-pay-dee-um]

Seize the day.
From the Roman poet Horace.

Don't put off until tomorrow
what you can do today.
Carpe diem.
Enjoy yourself; it is later than you think.

carte blanche

[cart-blonsh]

White card.
Unrestricted privilege.
Anything goes.
Otherwise expressed as a "blank check."

Germany gave Austria carte blanche in 1914.
The result was the First World War.

Cassandra

Cassandra was the daughter of
Priam and Hecuba.
Agamemnon brought her home as a prize
from the Trojan War.
She was a prophet cursed by Apollo to foretell
the truth but never to be believed.
Usually she foretold doom or disaster.
If you're a Cassandra it means you're
a doomsayer that no one takes seriously
until it is too late.

In the sequel to the film The Terminator,
*Linda Hamilton's character, who foretold
an apocalyptic war with machines,
was locked in a padded cell.
Unfortunately for her captors,
she turned out to be a Cassandra.*

castrato

[cah-strah-toh]

It sounds like what it is.
A male singer who is castrated before
reaching puberty in order to retain
his high, pure, boyish voice.

*Needless to say, you won't find many of these
around anymore, though the recent film* Farinelli,
*which portrayed the life of a castrato,
captured the public imagination.
These days, the men with high voices who
sing in choirs are called countertenors,
and their manhood, so to speak, is intact.*

casus belli

[cas-us-bell-ee]

A cause of war.
You can remember belli as the root
of the word bellicose, which means
eager to fight, pugnacious.

*The abduction of Helen of Troy was
the casus belli of the Trojan War.
Saddam Hussein's invasion of Kuwait
was the casus belli of the Gulf War.*

categorical imperative

Philosopher Immanuel Kant's term
for the binding moral law,
which states that one must act
according to maxims
that could serve as universal laws.

The following are categorical imperatives:
"Treat humanity as an end, never a means."
"Do unto others as you would
have them do unto you."

cause célèbre

[cause-sell-ebb-ruh]

Celebrated cause.
Sacred cow.
A person or event adopted by a political
party or other movement and given
symbolic meaning in public debate.

*Mumia Abu-Jamal, the ex-Black Panther
on death row, is a cause célèbre of the
American intellectual left, as were
Julius and Ethel Rosenberg in the 1950s.*

c'est la guerre

[say-la-gair]

Such is war.
Has come to mean "that's the way it goes"
or again in French, c'est la vie, "that's life."

When your cat vomits on your pillow,
to express your amused annoyance
at the vicissitudes of life, you might say,
"C'est la guerre."

chacun à son goût

[shack-un-ah-sawn-goo]

Each to his own taste.
Live and let live.
Often with a sarcastic undertone
insinuating disapproval.

*The incorrigible actress Tallulah Bankhead
said her own version of chacun à son goût when,
upon seeing the Catholic bishop of New York in full
regalia, traversing the aisle of St. Patrick's Cathedral,
and swinging the censer, she reputedly said,
"Honey, I love your dress, but your purse is on fire."*

chef-d'oeuvre

[shay-duh-vra]

Your chief or principal work.
A masterpiece.

magnum opus

Your greatest work.

*President Clinton's magnum opus was
supposed to be health care reform;
it ended up that his chef-d'oeuvre
was damage control.*

chiaroscuro

[key-are-o-scuro]

Light and dark.
Chiaro, light, and oscuro, dark, as in obscure.
A technique used most often in painting where the
contrast between light and dark is very stark.

*The sixteenth-century Italian baroque painter
Caravaggio was a master of chiaroscuro.*

Cleopatra's nose

The beauty of which caused Antony
to lose the Roman Empire.
Any folly of passion which incurs
great loss for a trifle.
Or, as Blaise Pascal wrote,
"Cleopatra's nose, had it been shorter,
the whole face of the world
would have changed."

*Edward VIII abdicated the English
throne to wed his inamorata,
the divorcée Wallis Simpson.
Once again, a kingdom lost
for Cleopatra's nose.*

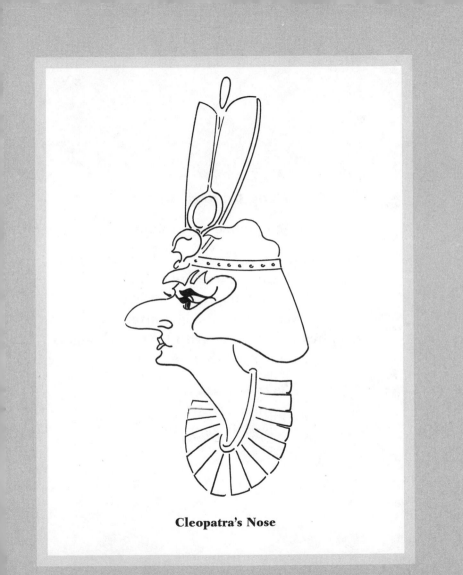

Cleopatra's Nose

cogito, ergo sum

[co-gee-toe-air-go-sum]

Philosopher René Descartes's famous phrase
"I think, therefore I am."
After systematically doubting
everything outside himself,
Descartes was left only with his own thoughts
as the proof that he existed.

*The candidate's arguments
were as airtight
as cogito, ergo sum.*

cognoscenti

[kan-ye-shen-tee]

The most informed members of any group.
Those who are in the know.
Cognizant of the most important facts
and fictions of high culture.

*If you want to join the cognoscenti,
learn what's in this book.*

comme il faut

[come-eel-foe]

As it must be.
As is proper.

*Prince Philip walks behind Queen Elizabeth,
comme il faut.*

compos mentis

[comp-os-meant-us]

Mentally competent.
Most often heard in last wills
and testaments where it is of utmost
importance that the will maker was of sound
mind when (s)he composed the will.

*Jeffrey Dahmer was found to be compos mentis,
and thus fit to stand trial.*

contretemps

[con-tra-tomp]

A misadventure or embarrassing situation.

*George Bush disgorging on the
Japanese prime minister
was a contretemps of the highest order.*

corpus delicti

[core-puss-dee-lick-tie]

The body of the crime, or the physical evidence.
Often the corpse in a murder case.

*In certain New York City murder cases,
when found in the Hudson,
the corpus delicti is affectionately
referred to as a "floater."*

coup d'état

[coo-day-tah]

A revolution or overthrow of state.
Often called a coup for short.

*In 1991 there was a coup d'état
in the Soviet Union that ended the Cold War.
The Communist empire crumbled and
democracy and free markets were
eventually installed, though economic
and political problems still abound.*

coup de foudre

[coo-duh-food-ra]

Bolt of lightning.
One often uses this when
referring to people who fall in love
at first sight, as though they've been
struck by lightning.

Cupid is the master of the coup de foudre.

coup de grâce

[coo-duh-grahs]

The final, often merciful death blow.

*When Sir Thomas More was beheaded
by order of King Henry VIII,
he tipped the executioner so as to ensure
a clean and quick coup de grâce.*

One tall decaf Coup d'etat, a latte Coup de grâce with cinnamon, and a short, skinny Coup de foudre.

cross the Rubicon

To cross the point of no return.
To take decisive action from which
there is no turning back.
The Rubicon is a river in northern Italy
that formed the border between the ancient
Roman republic and neighboring Gaul.
In 49 B.C., Julius Caesar crossed it with his
army and thereby began the ill-fated civil
war against Pompey.

*Hitler crossed his Rubicon when he invaded the
Soviet Union and broke his pact with Stalin.*

cum

[come]

with/become
Intelligent students often graduate
from college summa cum laude,
or with highest (summa) honors (laude).

*When he was elected mayor of Carmel,
California, Clint Eastwood was called
an actor cum politician.*

danse macabre

[donce-muh-kab-ruh]

Dance of death.
Medieval dance in which a skeleton
representing death led other skeletons
or living people to their graves.

*The annual Greenwich Village Halloween
parade in New York City is a festive re-creation
of a danse macabre.*

dark horse

The underdog in a contest.
From horse racing.
An unexpected or little known candidate.

*Elections are always more exciting when the dark
horse gives the incumbent a run for his money.*

de facto

[day-fact-o]

From according to the fact.
From according to reality.

de jure

[day-jur-ay]

According to the law.

*Some say OJ was innocent de jure,
but guilty de facto.*

dementia praecox

[duh-men-shuh-pree-cox]

Premature madness.
In his play *Suddenly Last Summer*,
Tennessee Williams
uses this phrase to describe the madness
of one of his characters.
(You might also see the phrase ejaculato
praecox, which in the interests of good taste
needn't be defined here. Suffice it to say,
it's a problem that a castrato never has.)

In Alfred Hitchcock's film Psycho,
Norman Bates suffered from dementia praecox.

dénouement

[day-new-mah]

The undoing of a knot.
The final unraveling or completion of a plot.

Shakespeare's Hamlet *has a stunning
and sanguinary dénouement.*

de rigueur

[duh-ree-grrr]

Obligatory.
What is done.
Required by current custom or fashion.

*It's de rigueur to wash your hands
after using the W.C.*

desideratum

[deh-sid-er-ot-um]

Something wished for, needed, or desired.

The missing link was Darwin's desideratum.

détente

[day-taunt]

The mechanism in a crossbow by which
the string is released.
The easing of strained relations.

*On the eve of World War II, British prime minister
Neville Chamberlain finagled a détente with
Hitler, and naively declared he had achieved,
"peace in our time."*

deus ex machina

[day-us-ex-mock-ee-nuh]

God from the machine.
A theatrical ploy used in ancient
Greek tragedy in which a god appeared at
the end of the play to solve the problems
of the main characters.
The god descended from the
sky on a kind of crane.

*If you are accused of invoking the
deus ex machina it means that you have taken
the easy way out of resolving your plot,
instead of making your characters come to
real terms with the troubles you have unfolded.*

dharma

[darm-uh]

That which binds and sustains.

*In Hinduism, dharma is a sacred law
of society denoting moral order.
In Buddhism, dharma is the law of Buddha,
the basic doctrine of the Four Noble Truths,
and one of the Three Jewels of the faith.*

Dr. Johnson's Boot

This is one of the all-time great philosophical refutations, famous for its wit and incisiveness. The philosopher George Berkeley was known for his theory that nothing material existed in the world. It was called idealism, and according to it, everything in the world that seemed physical was nothing more than an idea in the mind. Dr. Samuel Johnson, the great eighteenth-century moralist, lexicographer, and essayist, upon hearing about Berkeley's theory proclaimed it absurd. One day while out walking, he offered his official refutation. He kicked a stone that was lying in his path and said, "I refute it thus."

The philosopher's prose had the bluntness and refreshing good sense of Dr. Johnson's Boot.

Dr. Johnson's Boot

donnybrook

A brawl, uproar, or fight.
Named after the Donnybrook Fair in Ireland,
which was noted for its uproariousness.

*The debate over intelligent design (creationism)
and random mutation (Darwinism) is an ongoing
donnybrook in scientific circles.*

Doppelgänger

[dop-ul-gang-ur]

Double-walker.
A double or twin, often pernicious,
ghostly or haunting.

*Someone who steals your identity,
drains your bank account, and maxes out your
credit cards is your Doppelgänger.*

dramatis personae

[drom-at-iss-per-son-ay]

The list of characters that usually appears
at the beginning of a play, but can also be used
in other forms of fiction and nonfiction as a way
of identifying the major players in the drama
and providing necessary background
information about them.

In any given production of A Doll's House,
*you can find out who played Torvald
by referring to the dramatis personae.*

droit du seigneur

[dwa-doo-say-nure]

Any right owed to the local lord.
One of the most outlandish such privileges of the
Middle Ages was that of prima noche, the right of
the feudal lord to bed the brides of his vassals the
night before they were married.

*Some have quipped that Bill Clinton thought
he was exercising his droit du seigneur when
he called Paula Jones to his hotel room.*

ecce homo

[eck-ay-homo]

"Behold the man."
The infamous phrase Pontius Pilate uttered as
he presented Jesus to the Jews before crucifixion.

élan vital

[eh-lon-vee-tall]

Vital force.
Life force.
Popularized by the French philosopher
Henri Bergson.

*When he sang in the rain, Gene Kelly
demonstrated his elegant brand of élan vital.*

embonpoint

[um-bawn-pwain]

Literally, in good condition.
Plump. Chubby.

*Sarah Ferguson, who was dubbed "full-figured"
by the British tabloids, was indeed a little
embonpoint when she married Prince Andrew.*

éminence grise

[em-ee-nonce-greez]

Gray eminence.
A person who wields power
from behind the scenes.
Originally it referred to Père Joseph,
secretary to the French Cardinal Richelieu.

The caustic New Yorker *film critic
Anthony Lane once made a witty play on this
phrase when he referred to the now obese Marlon
Brando as the éminence grosse, or "fat éminence,"
of the film* Don Juan de Marco.

Éminence Grise

enfant terrible

[ehn-font-tare-ee-blah]

Terrible child.
A talented young upstart who breaks the rules.

In Hollywood, James Dean was the
enfant terrible of his time.

ennui

[on-we]

Existential boredom.
Coined by the French existentialists.
The colossal, mind-numbing, soul-crushing
boredom of believing that there is no God
and no reasoned order in the universe.

Most downtowners in New York City feel ennui
whenever they venture above Fourteenth Street.

épater le bourgeoisie

[eh-pat-ay-le-boor-jwa-zee]

Shock the middle class.
Attributed to the nineteenth-century
French poet Charles Baudelaire.

*In an article about the mainstreaming
of gay life, writer Daniel Mendelsohn made
a skillful play on this expression when he said gays
were so eager to seem normal that instead of
shocking, they were "aping the bourgeoisie."*

erratum

[air-ah-tum]

Error.

A copy editor corrects an erratum in a manuscript.

esprit de corps

[ess-pree-duh-core]

Spirit of the body.
The mood of a group.
Togetherness. Solidarity.

*In boot camp, drill instructors are
determined to instill in recruits an
ironclad and boisterous esprit de corps.*

Et tu Brute?

[ett-two-brute-ay]

"And you also, Brutus?"

Julius Caesar said this to his trusted confidant
Brutus as he was being stabbed by him.
It expressed Caesar's surprise, disappointment,
and sadness at discovering that his friend
was among his betrayers.

exempli gratia (e.g.)

[egg-zem-plee-gra-tee-uh]

For example.

Some things can never be found fresh—e.g., sardines.

ex nihilo

[ex-nee-hill-oh]

Out of nothing.
God's creation of everything in the universe,
including Himself, out of nothingness.
Thus, God is known in ancient Greek and
medieval philosophy as the First Cause,
or the thing that created itself.

*Every writer faces that proverbial blank page
and must create his/her work ex nihilo.*

ex parte

[ex-par-tay]

From one side. Partisan.

In political debates, the participants argue ex parte.

ex post facto

[ex-post-fact-toe]

After the fact.
Something that is done retroactively but
with reference to something that came before.

*If your pay raise doesn't start showing up
on your paycheck for three months, you'll get
a lump sum in the fourth month for the
amount not paid you during the first three
months. That's a payment ex post facto.*

ex tempore

[ex-tem-pour-ay]

Outside time. Spontaneously.
The related English verb is extemporize.

*At weddings, friends and relatives
are often asked to give toasts to the
bride and groom ex tempore.*

fait accompli

[fete-a-com-plee]

An action that is already completed.
A done deal.

*Spilled milk is a fait accompli,
so why cry over it?*

fatwa

[faht-wah]

A Muslim declaration of a death sentence.

In 1989, the Ayatollah Khomeini declared a fatwa against the British writer Salman Rushdie for the alleged blasphemy of his book The Satanic Verses.

Faustian pact

Deal with the devil.

Faust was the protagonist, if he can be called such, in the German writer Goethe's classic play of the same name. Faust sold his soul to the devil, Mephistopheles, in exchange for youth and the fulfillment of his yearning to experience all the world. Many plays, books, musicals, and films have adopted this theme, including the 1950s musical *Damn Yankees*, Boito's opera *Mefistofele*, and Gounod's opera *Faust*.

Luciano Pavarotti is such a phenomenally good singer, you'd almost suspect he'd made a Faustian pact in his youth.

faute de mieux

[fote-duh-mee-uh]

Lack of a better.
You take what is at hand because
there is nothing better around.

*The rock band Crosby, Stills, Nash & Young said
their version of faute de mieux when they sang:
"If you can't be with the one you love,
love the one you're with."*

faux pas

[foe-pah]

False step.
A social error.
Something unacceptable.

*It is de rigueur to wear black to funerals.
It would be a faux pas to wear hot pink.*

Festschrift

[fest-shrift]

A collection of essays written
by colleagues and/or students
in honor of a scholar.

*Upon his retirement from the university,
students and colleagues of the revered
philosophy professor compiled
a Festschrift in his honor.*

figure in the carpet

The title of a short story by Henry James.
It refers to that which is buried
or hidden within something else.
A subtext.

Or, as James himself wrote:
"Vereker's secret . . . the general
intention of his books:
the string the pearls were strung on,
the buried treasure; the figure in the carpet."

fin de siècle

[fan-duh-see-eck-luh]

Of or pertaining to the end of the
nineteenth century.
In general it can mean the end of an era.

*Surfing the Internet is the sport of the
twentieth-century fin de siècle.*

flagrante delicto

[flah-grahn-tay-duh-lick-toe]

Caught in the act.
Originally in the act of committing a crime,
but often referring to sex.

*Gary Hart was caught in flagrante
delicto with Donna Rice.*

force majeure

[force-mah-jure]

Superior or magnificent force.
This phrase often appears in contracts
between authors and publishers. It refers
to so-called "acts of God"or other
catastrophic events, like earthquakes,
that are beyond human control.
The clause ensures that in case of such
disasters, the usual deadlines and
provisos of a contract are suspended.

Hurricane Andrew was a force majeure.

fourth estate

Journalists, the press, the media.

*Edmund Burke coined the term when he said,
"Yonder sits the fourth estate, more important
than them all."
The first three estates are the clergy
(the Lords Spiritual), the barons and knights
(the Lords Temporal), and the Commons.*

Frankfurt School

The Marxist school of the 1920s and 1930s
that centered on the Institute for Social
Research in Frankfurt led by Max Horkheimer,
Theodor Adorno, Herbert Marcuse,
Walter Benjamin, and Jürgen Habermas.
In their teaching, known as "critical theory,"
they argued that a combination of aesthetics,
psychoanalysis, and popular culture reinforced
the prevailing Western condition of passive,
depersonalized acceptance of the status quo.

Frankfurt School

gang aft a-gley

Even the most careful planning often fails
to make things go smoothly.
From the eighteenth-century Scottish
poet Robert Burns's poem *To a Mouse:*

*"The best laid schemes o' mice an' men
Gang aft a-gley"* [often go astray.]

Gemütlichkeit

[geh-moot-lick-ite]

That cozy, homey,
warm-by-the-hearth kind of feeling
you get in your grandmother's
kitchen—unless you're Sybil.

*Barbara Bush brought Gemütlichkeit
to the White House.*

gerrymander

To divide into voting districts, or manipulate district zones in order to give unfair advantage to one party in elections. Named after Elbridge Gerry, who was governor of Massachusetts in 1812.

Gerrymandering undermines true democracy.

Gestalt

[guh-shtahlt]

A whole is more than the sum of its parts. A German concept later used to define a school of analysis called Gestalt psychology.

Gestalt thinkers usually miss the trees for the forest.

ghost in the machine

A sarcastic reference to the nature of the mind/body relationship according to Cartesian dualism, spit out by the English philosopher Gilbert Ryle. According to Ryle, if there is no connection between the mind and the body, then the mind is just like a free floating ghost in that machine we call our body.

When Hal, the supercomputer in 2001 A Space Odyssey, *malfunctioned and refused to obey commands, "he," like a ghost in the machine, took on a life of his own.*

glasnost

[glass-nohst]

Openness—especially social and political.
The term was popularized by Soviet premier
Mikail Gorbachev, who used it to express his
commitment to razing the all but impermeable
walls of Soviet secrecy in government and its
iron-fisted control of its populace.
(See perestroika)

*Glasnost was the beginning
of the end for the USSR.*

Gongorism

[gon-gor-iz-um]

A Spanish literary style that is pompous in its overbearing use of Latin terms and arcane references to Greek mythology. Named after the seventeenth-century Spanish poet Luis de Góngora who used this technique to enrich his works. Lesser modern poets have used it as a kind of affectation that stinks of pretension for its own sake.

Readers put off by his erudition
have said that T. S. Eliot
was guilty of Gongorism.

Gordian knot

An intricate problem.
It is named after Gordias, king of Phrygia,
who dedicated his wagon to Zeus.
(God knows why.)
The yoke of the wagon was tied to a pole
so intricately that it was said that whoever undid
the knot would reign over the Asian empire.
Alexander cut the knot with one blow.

If you've cut the Gordian knot,
you've solved a difficult problem decisively.

habeas corpus

[hab-ee-us-core-puss]

Produce the body.
A writ or court order that allows a prisoner to be brought before a judge in order that he might be released from unlawful custody.

In one hilarious demonstration of his surprising and delightful acumen, Bugs Bunny shouted, "Habeas corpus" ad nauseam when he was thrown into prison by an exasperated Yosemite Sam.

halcyon days

[hal-see-on-days]

Carefree times of calm, peace, and prosperity.
Halcyon is the Greek word for kingfisher:
hals, the sea and *kyo*, to brood on.
Sicilian sailors believed that the halcyon made
their nests on the sea during the winter solstice
and had the power to calm the surf.
Those nesting days became known
as halcyon days.

*Summers on Martha's Vineyard
are filled with halcyon days.*

hara-kiri

[hahra-keeree]

Japanese ritual suicide by disembowelment.

In the film Harold and Maude, *the eccentric young man, Harold, who is in love with an eighty-year-old woman, chases away one of the girls his mother wants him to marry by simulating hara-kiri in front of her.*

hauteur

[oh-tur]

Haughtiness. Arrogance.

Shyness can often be mistaken for hauteur.

hobgoblin

A goblin, imp, or misbehaving elf.

The nineteenth-century American essayist Ralph Waldo Emerson wrote, "A foolish consistency is the hobgoblin of little minds."

Hobson's choice

A choice between equally bad alternatives. After Thomas Hobson, an English horse boarder, who told his customers that they had to take the horse nearest the stable door, or none at all.

When asked who she was going to vote for in the 1996 Presidential election, Clinton or Dole, Joan Rivers made a clever quip about what she considered a Hobson's choice:

"It's like trying to choose your favorite Menendez brother."

hoi polloi

[hoy-pull-oy]

The people.
The masses, the many.
Hoi means "the" in Greek, so don't be an
ignoramus and say, "the hoi polloi."

*Popular culture is directed by hoi polloi
through the box office.*

hoist with his own petar[d]

Blown up by his own bomb.
When you are killed by your own weapon,
or ruined by your own evil schemes.
From Shakespeare's *Hamlet*:
"They must sweep my way and marshal
me to knavery. Let it work; for 'tis the
sport to have the enginer hoist with
his own petar."

*Because he was greedy and broke
his promises, the Machiavellian
English king Richard III was hoist
with his own petard when he was
defeated by the armies of his
erstwhile conspirators.*

homo faber

[ho-mo-fah-bear]

Man the maker.

Expresses the atheistic predisposition to emphasize the creative power of man over that of an unseen creator-god.
A novel by Max Frisch that captures the existential anguish of modern man.
His narrator explains:
"I don't believe in providence and fate, as a technologist I am used to reckoning with the formulas of probability."

Hottentot

Libertine or sexual free spirit.
The Hottentot Venus was the name given
to an African girl of the Hottentot tribe who was
captured, brought to England, and put on display
because she had abnormally large buttocks.
She came to symbolize fertility and unrestrained
sexuality to the rather uptight British aristocracy,
who viewed her as a freak of nature.

Madonna is a hopeless Hottentot.

hubris

[hue-briss]

Overweening pride.
Arrogance.

*It was pure hubris to think the Titanic was
unsinkable, and thus her sinking was to many
like a Greek tragedy, a punishment from the gods.*

idée fixe

[ee-day-fix]

An obsession or fixation.
In music, a repeated theme or strain of melody
that evokes the mood of the piece.

*Ponce de León's idée fixe
was the fountain of youth.*

id est (i.e.)

That is.
An abbreviation used to clarify or flesh out
a point that has already been made.
Akin to the English phrase "that is to say."

*As Nancy Reagan admonished,
drugs are bad, i.e., "Just say no."*

in absentia

[in-ab-sen-cha]

Not present. A fancy way of saying absent.

If you're talking to your brother's fiancée on the phone over Thanksgiving, you might say, "Welcome to our family, in absentia."

inamorata/inamorato

[i-na-more-a-ta]

The woman/man with whom you are enamored or in love.

Juliet was Romeo's inamorata.

incommunicado

[in-com-yu-nick-ah-do]

Not in communication, not reachable.

*On safari in the depths of the African jungle, you are likely incommunicado.
Unless you have your cellular.*

in loco parentis

[in-low-ko-pah-ren-tiss]

In place of parents.

When you were a child your baby-sitter functioned in loco parentis when your parents went to the theater on Saturday nights.

in medias res

[in-mee-dee-us-ress]

In the middle of.
Something that begins
in the middle of the action.

Schwarzenegger films often begin in medias res with a car chase, a love scene, or a shootout.

In Search of Lost Time

A seven-part novel by the early twentieth-century French writer Marcel Proust. Included here lest you make the unforgivable faux pas of referring to it by the common title. The French title, *A la récherche du temps perdu*, is most often translated as *Remembrance of Things Past*, which is in fact not a faithful translation, but rather a catchy line from Shakespeare's Sonnet 30:

"When to the sessions of sweet silent thought, I summon up remembrance of things past . . ."

inter alia

[in-tur-ahl-ee-uh]

Among other things.

Raisins go into a fruitcake, inter alia.

in vino veritas

[in-vee-no-vare-ee-tahs]

In wine there is truth.
Used by Plato in his *Symposium*.
It means you tend to tell the truth,
for better or worse, when you're drunk.
Ring any bells?

*Accosted by Lady Astor, who spluttered,
"Winston Churchill, you're drunk,"
the prime minister replied, "Yes I am, but in the
morning I'll be sober, and you'll still be ugly."*

ipso facto

By the fact.

A columnist who writes for
The Nation *or* The Weekly Standard, *ipso facto,*
has no right to call herself objective.

ivory tower

In everyday speech this refers to the privileged isolation of academic life at certain elite universities and colleges. It is something of a sneering remark since it implies that academics don't really live in the real world, but instead inhabit an irrelevant realm of books and useless ideas.

In ivory towers across America, debates are still raging over what constitutes the Western canon.

Ivory Tower

jabberwocky

Nonsense.
Gibberish. From Lewis Carroll's
gibberish-speaking Jabberwock in
Through the Looking Glass.

Dan Quayle was a master of jabberwocky.

j'accuse

[jah-kyuze]

I accuse.
Denotes a formal and public accusation.
A feuilleton (pamphlet) by the French novelist
Émile Zola published in 1898.
It was a public indictment of the anti-Semitic
persecutors of the French army officer
Alfred Dreyfus, for which Zola was prosecuted
for libel and later pardoned.
Dreyfus was falsely accused of betraying military
secrets to Germany in 1894, court-martialed,
and sent to Devil's Island prison.
He was exonerated in 1906 due in large
part to the call to arms sounded by Zola.

Jacobins

Extremist republicans of the French Revolution,
who proclaimed the French Republic
and executed the king.
Through the Committee of Public Safety,
led by Danton and Robespierre,
they began the Reign of Terror.

jeremiad

[jare-uh-my-add]

A long lament.
From Jeremiah in the Old Testament,
who endured long and arduous
imprisonment and suffering.

*After their misdeeds were made public,
Jim and Tammy Faye Baker entertained America
with their teary jeremiad.*

Jezebel

[jez-ih-bell]

In the Old Testament, the power-hungry,
scheming, temptress wife of Ahab.

*Nowadays, if someone calls you a Jezebel,
it usually means not only that you're brash,
but also that you're something of a harlot.*

jihad

[jee-hahd]

Declaration of a holy war.

*Other Arab nations feared Saddam Hussein would
declare a jihad in the Gulf War and put undue
pressure on their Muslim citizens to bear arms
against the United States.*

joie de vivre

[jwa de veev-ruh]

Joy of life.

A certain talent for living, which allows
enjoyment of the little things.
A sparkling, contagious happiness.

Bette Midler is famous for her joie de vivre.

junta

[hoon-tah]

A group, usually military, that
comes to power after a revolution.

In his novel Eleni, *Nicholas Gage tells the story
of his childhood in Greece after World War II, and
how his mother was tortured and killed at the hands
of the Communist junta that took over their village.*

laissez-faire

[lay-say-fair]

Let be. Let go.
Originated with the Physiocrats, a group of
eighteenth-century French economists whose
maxim was, "laissez-faire et laissez-passer"
"let go and let pass."
Popularized by the economist Adam Smith
in his treatise *The Wealth of Nations*, it often
means a policy, whether economic or political,
of letting things go their own course without
official intervention.

Reaganomics was laissez-faire capitalism.

Lebensraum

[lay-benz-raum]

Living room.

*Lebensraum was the Nazi excuse for the
invasion of Poland in 1939.
Ostensibly, they needed more space to live in.*

le mot juste

[luh-mo-juiced]

Exactly the right word.
More specifically, it means the best,
the one and only word that is appropriate
for a certain situation.

*Dorothy Parker always came up with le mot juste.
Once at a fancy tea with society ladies, Parker
was asked to take part in a game in which each
person was given a "big" word to use correctly
in a sentence. Parker hated pretentious society
ladies, so when she got her word, which was
"horticulture," she said, "You can lead a
horticulture, but you can't make her think."*

lèse-majesté

[lez-maj-es-tay]

The outrage of not giving majesty its due.
A crime or offense that shows disrespect for
a ruler or other high-ranking person.
Lytton Strachey's book *Eminent Victorians*,
in which he criticized and ridiculed the English
upper class, was a classic example of lèse-majesté.

libretto

[lib-ret-oh]

The lyrics in an opera score.

The poet W. H. Auden wrote the libretto
for Stravinsky's opera *The Rake's Progress*.

lingua franca

[ling-gwa-fron-ca]

French tongue.
Common language.
Ironically, *Lingua Franca* is also the name of
an uncommonly highbrow academic journal.

English is the lingua franca of the United Nations.
Money is the lingua franca of business.
Music is the lingua franca of love.

literati

[lit-ur-ot-ee]

The literary crowd.
Intelligentsia.

In the 1920s, Virginia Woolf and the Bloomsbury Group were the most famous literati of their generation.

"I'll take a pound of literati, a half-pound
of paparazzi and a slice of cognoscenti."

litmus test

Any means of dividing people
into two distinct groups.
Litmus paper is used to test degrees
of acidity in chemicals.
You may remember giving it to your friends
to taste so that you could conduct an experiment
in high school science. Some people tasted acid,
others tasted nothing.
A litmus test, then, is something that separates
people or things into categories.

*The words in this book could be considered
a litmus test for whether or not you are
a cultured, educated person.*

Lost Generation

Anyone who came of age during and
just after World War I.

*The 1920s expatriate Parisians, including
Ernest Hemingway and F. Scott Fitzgerald,
were befriended by the grande dame of
American letters, Gertrude Stein,
who dubbed them the "Lost Generation."*

lotus-eater

Someone who lives in idle luxury.
According to Homer's *Odyssey*, a people
who ate the lotus tree, which had the effect
of making them forget everything and
lose all desire to return home.

*To its detractors, the British royal family
is a clan of lotus-eaters.*

Luddite

Someone opposed to technological progress. From the nineteenth-century movement that disapproved of labor-saving devices.

The Unabomber is the most notorious Luddite of our times.

Luftmensch

[luft-mensh]

A person with his or her head in the clouds. A dreamer.

Goethe's character Werther, the protagonist in his novel The Sorrows of Young Werther, *was the prototypical Luftmensch.*

Lumpenproletariat

[lump-in-pro-lit-air-ee-at]

Any disenfranchised group.
In philosopher Karl Marx's *Das Kapital*,
Lumpenproletariat were the bottom-rung
working class who lacked class solidarity.

*Rogue politician Pat Buchanan is the self-styled
champion of the American Lumpenproletariat.*

"I regret to inform you that we have found a Lumpenproletariat."

Machiavellian

[mock-ee-uh-vell-ee-an]

The sixteenth-century Florentine statesman
and political philosopher Niccolò Machiavelli
wrote a small book called *The Prince*.
He offered it to a younger member of the Medicis,
the Florentine ruling family, intending it to be a
guidebook on how to acquire and keep power.
If you follow Machiavelli's advice, you're
scheming and ruthless, a power hungry,
manipulative person who will do what it takes
to win or rule, as the case may be.

Richard Nixon was Machiavellian.

Machiavellian

malapropos

[mal-ah-prop-oh]

Badly to the purpose.
Inappropriate.
In his comic play *The Rivals*, the
eighteenth-century Irish playwright
Richard Brinsley Sheridan named one
of his characters Mrs. Malaprop,
for her tendency to spout malapropisms,
or misused words, whose multisyllabic
impressiveness she enjoyed, but whose true
meanings she didn't understand. Hence,
her propensity for shouting things like:

*"She's as headstrong as an allegory
on the banks of the Nile."*

mammon

From the New Testament,
it means money or wealth.
From Matthew's Gospel,
"No man can serve two masters . . .
Ye cannot serve God and mammon."

*The New York Stock Exchange is often
called the temple of mammon.*

manna from heaven

In the Old Testament, the food miraculously
supplied to the Children of Israel during the
forty years wandering in the desert.
What they thought was God's gift is now
thought to have been the excrement of
insects who fed on desert trees.
Any unexpected gift or good grace.

Rain on a sweltering day is manna from heaven.

maquis

[mock-ee]

The French Resistance of World War II.
Commonly used to describe any underground
subversive group.

The IRA could be called a maquis.
The London Underground could not.

marianismo

[mary-anne-is-mo]

The opposite of machismo. The superiority of the female over the male, especially spiritually.

It is often said that marriage between a man and a woman is good because marianismo has a civilizing influence on men.

mea culpa

[may-uh-cull-puh]

I am culpable.

If the waitress spills scalding coffee on you and she is a moonlighting graduate student, she might say, "Oh, mea culpa."

memento mori

[mem-ent-o-moree]

A reminder of mortality.

*In her novel of the same name, Muriel Spark told
the story of an old woman who kept receiving
prank phone calls from someone who said only,
"Remember you must die," and hung up.
Shakespeare included a gentle
memento mori in his play* Cymbeline:

*"Golden lads and girls all must
like chimney sweepers come to dust."*

ménage à trois

[may-noj-ah-twa]

A household where three people live together.
Any intimate combination of three people. It is
often taken to imply a lewd arrangement that has
more to do with hand-holds than households.

*The Marquis de Sade was fond
of a good ménage à trois.*

mensch

[mensh]

Man.
In Yiddish it denotes a true, good human being. A mensch does the right thing, or the generous thing when other people would not.

A mensch would lend his friend $100 even when nearly broke himself.

milquetoast

[milk-toast]

A person with a meek, cowering disposition.
A comic-strip character created by
H. T. Webster in the 1950s.

*Henpeckers usually have
milquetoast husbands.*

mise-en-scène

[meez-un-sen]

A set.
The placement of actors and props on a stage.
An environment in general.

The wretched excess of the 1920s provided
the mise-en-scène for the crash of 1929.

modus operandi

[mo-dus-op-er-on-die]

Method or way of operating.

modus vivendi

[mo-dus-viv-en-dee]

Method or way of living.

Many a courtesan has developed a modus operandi of courting the rich and powerful in order to support a lavish modus vivendi.

Mrs. Grundy

The powerful censorship exerted in everyday
life by the influence of conventional wisdom
and received opinion.
A character in Thomas Morton's 1798 play
Speed the Plough, who never appears onstage
but with whom Dame Ashfield is obsessed,
constantly worrying,
"What would Mrs. Grundy think . . ."

Don't worry about Mrs. Grundy,
go ahead and marry the pool boy.

Mrs. Grundy

music of the spheres

According to the ancient Greek mathematician Pythagoras, all the planets orbited in perfect harmony and vibrated, also in musical harmony, according to their different rates of movement, inevitably producing celestial music.

For astrologists, the music of the spheres is the voice of destiny.

nabob

A Hindi term for a man of wealth and power.

*The French nineteenth-century novelist
Honoré de Balzac wrote, among other things,
of harlots and dancers who were kept
secretly by nabobs—usually members
of the Parisian aristocracy.*

nebbish

A timid, weak person of
little consequence.

*Until he ate his spinach,
Popeye was a nebbish.*

nirvana

[nerve-on-ah]

The state of complete blessedness in Buddhism.
The end of the cycle of reincarnations
attained through the abandonment
of the ego or self.
An ideal condition of harmony and bliss.

To Timothy Leary, LSD was nirvana.

"I will take a one-way ticket to nirvana, please."

noble savage

The paragon of unspoiled man
in a state of nature.
From Jean-Jacques Rousseau.

In his Leatherstocking Tales, *nineteenth-century
American novelist James Fenimore Cooper told the
story of the American frontier in upstate New York.
His hero, Natty Bumpo, is the quintessential
noble savage, or moral tough guy who
grew up in the woods.*

noblesse oblige

[no-bless-oh-bleej]

Noble obligation.
Honorable or courtly behavior on the part
of well-born or high-ranking people.

*In the age of political correctness,
noblesse oblige is an odious concept.*

noli me tangere

[no-lee-me-tahn-jer-eh]

Touch me not.
A thing that should not be touched.
A term for any picture of Jesus appearing to
Mary Magdalene after the Resurrection.

*Some academic tomes are so difficult to decipher,
they might as well have "noli me tangere"
printed on the cover.*

nom de guerre

[num-duh-gare]

Name of war.
Your battle name.

*Bill Clinton's nom de guerre, the Comeback Kid,
reenergized a stalled presidency.*

nom de plume

[num-duh-ploom]

Your pen name.

Voltaire was the nom de plume of Jean-François Marie Arouet. George Eliot was the nom de plume of Mary Ann Evans.

nomenklatura

[no-men-kla-tur-ah]

The elite in Soviet bureaucracy.
The opposite of apparatchiks.
A close relative in English is nomenclature,
which means the cant or jargon of a profession.

New Soviet leaders were always chosen
from the nomenklatura.
Medical nomenclature includes terms like
rhinoplasty, which is Latin for nose job.

non sequitur

[non-sek-wi-tur]

Does not follow.
Something unrelated to or unproven
by whatever came before.

*The verbiage of schizophrenics is often
replete with non sequiturs.*

nota bene (n.b.)

[note-ah-ben-eh]

Note well.

*n.b. Mind your head when
descending the stairs.*

Occam's razor

The fourteenth-century English philosopher
William of Occam's famous principle
of simplicity in logic.
"Entities should not be multiplied
beyond what is needed."
In general, it's a method of simplifying
terminology and expression in the same
way you might cancel out equivalent terms
in a math problem.
Killing two birds with one stone.
The simpler, the better.

omertà

[oh-mare-tah]

The code of secrecy and silence
in the Sicilian mafia.

*Those who violate the omertà can expect
to pay for it with their lives.*

onomatopoeia

[on-oh-ma-to-pee-ah]

The quality of sounding like what it means.

Bang, smack, and slam are onomatopoeic.

outré

[oo-tray]

Beyond. Bizarre. Eccentric.

As far as nannies go,
Mary Poppins was rather outré.

Owl of Minerva

Wisdom.

"The Owl of Minerva spreads its wings only
with the coming of the dusk."—Hegel

Wisdom that comes at the end of the day.
Knowledge after the fact."Now *you tell me . . .*"

"What Youth deemed crystal,
Age finds out was dew."—Robert Browning

pace

[pah-chay]

Peace. With deference to.
With all due respect to.
Used to express polite disagreement.

*Pace your colleagues at the office,
you probably wouldn't be caught dead
with any of them after five* P.M.

palimpsest

An oily skin that could be wiped clean
of what was already written on it and
readied to be written on again.

*The acclaimed American writer Gore Vidal's
memoir was appropriately called* Palimpsest.

panache

[pon-ah-shh]

Flair. Charm. Personality. Style.
At the end of the play *Cyrano de Bergerac*,
by the nineteenth-century French playwright
Edmond Rostand, the story of a charming,
witty man with an enormous, ugly nose,
Cyrano says "J'ai encore mon panache."
I still have my plume or feather, referring
to the feather he wore in his cap, that
came to symbolize his scintillating and
effervescent personality.

Cary Grant had irrepressible panache.

Panglossian

Indomitably optimistic.
Dr. Pangloss was the tutor in Voltaire's *Candide*
who, even in the face of life's worst difficulties,
asserted vociferously that, "All is for the best in
this best of all possible worlds."

Dostoyevsky was not Panglossian.

paparazzi

[pop-ah-rots-ee]

Opportunistic photojournalists—
the kind who have no qualms about
rushing in to snap shots of topless starlets
and murdered gangsters.

In his 1960 film *La Dolce Vita*, Frederico Fellini
named the obnoxious photographer character
Paparazzo, meaning "little bug."

*The paparazzi were blamed by many
for the high-speed chase and the resulting
car accident that killed Diana Spencer,
the former Princess of Wales.*

pari passu

[par-ee-pass-oo]

With equal application to.
At an equal pace.
Fairly.

*The law applies pari passu to both the great
and the small, the rich and the poor.
Sure.*

pas de deux

[pa-duh-duh]

A duet, or dance for two in ballet.

*Mussolini and Hitler danced
a brief pas de deux.*

pastiche

[pa-steesh]

A pasted-together collection.
A hodgepodge, collage.

*The evening news is often a harried
pastiche of the day's events.*

pathetic fallacy

A dramatic device by which human characteristics
are given to inanimate things incapable of them;
when nature acts in sympathy with man.

*If a novel says that the trees drooped in sadness,
the sky wept, and the ocean fumed, the writer was
making liberal use of pathetic fallacy.*

patois

[pa-twa]

An accent, special jargon,
or dialect of a particular people.

*People from Louisiana are often said to
have a patois, which arose from the mixture
of African and French influences on the
language and culture.
Likewise, Jamaicans are often said
to speak a patois of English.*

pentimento

A repentance or correction.
The reappearance in a painting of an
earlier design that was painted over.
As old paintings fade, sometimes there
emerges an earlier image that the artist
eventually covered over.

*Currently, X-rays being done on several
Gainsboroughs have revealed pentimentos
of a series of dogs who once were included
in the paintings of their owners.
Appropriately enough, the American playwright
Lillian Hellman's memoir is called* Pentimento.

perestroika

[pair-uh-stroy-ka]

Soviet policy of economic and social reform.
Also used by Soviet premier Mikhail Gorbachev
as a term for the social and economic changes that
would flow from greater openness (glasnost)
to the world community, and fewer strictures on
the lives of a Soviet people so long ruled by fear.

*Sovietologists often claim that perestroika
was the crack in the Soviet colossus that
eventually brought it crashing down.*

per se

[per-say]

By itself. Intrinsically.

For most people, coffee, per se, is not particularly tasty. It needs the mitigation of cream and sugar.

persona non grata

[per-so-nah-non-gra-tah]

Someone who is unwelcome, out of favor, or disliked.

Dick Morris, once the leading strategist of the Clinton administration, became persona non grata at the White House once his alleged indiscretions were revealed.

philistine

[fill-ist-een]

An ignorant, ill-behaved, uncultured person. In the Old Testament, the Philistines were the enemies of the Israelites fought against by the Jewish heroes Samson and David. Matthew Arnold supposedly popularized the modern term by borrowing from the German term Philister, which means "outsiders," and which German university students used as a derogatory name for townspeople.

Philistines are American tourists who ask the French kiosk salesman how much his merchandise is in "real money."

pièce de résistance

[pee-es-duh-raise-ee-stons]

An outstanding accomplishment.

Michelangelo's David.
Tchaikovsky's Swan Lake.
Géricault's Raft of the Medusa.

pied-à-terre

[pee-ed-ah-tare]

Foot on the earth.
Usually a small apartment or office that is not
your primary residence or place of business,
but serves as a convenient stopover.

*If you live on Long Island, you might buy
a small studio in Greenwich Village
as your pied-à-terre in New York.*

poetic justice

Just deserts.
What goes around comes around.
The condition of getting
what is coming to you.

In his film The Magnificent Ambersons,
*Orson Welles expressed the essence of poetic
justice when he said that his protagonist,
the arrogant Harry Amberson, finally got
his "comeuppance" when he lost
everything dear to him.*

prima facie

[pre-muh-face-ee-uh]

At first sight.
Before closer inspection.

*Among callow Californians, a person
who is attractive prima facie but not from
closer up is known as a Monet.
Like the impressionist painter's Waterlilies,
such a person is beautiful from afar
and up close, a mess.*

primus inter pares

[pre-muhs-in-ter-par-is]

First among equals.

*Speaker of the House Newt Gingrich is
prima inter pares among members of Congress.*

pro bono

For the good.

*Most law firms donate some of their efforts
to clients unable to pay as a contribution to the
greater good of the communtiy.
Such cases are referred to as pro bono.*

pro forma

According to form.
Done in the way things are habitually done.

*Madeleine Albright's confirmation
hearings for Secretary of State were pro forma,
because they went the way hearings should,
formally, and without a hitch.*

putsch

[put-shh]

A revolution, coup, overthrow of government,
or plan to do such.

Hitler's Beer Hall Putsch, 1923.

Pyrrhic victory

[peer-ick-victory]

Empty victory.
A victory that is accompanied by overwhelming
losses. A battle that is won, but at such
great cost, with so many casualties,
that in truth it was no victory at all.
From the victory of Pyrrhus, King of Epirus
over the Romans at Asculum in 279 B.C.

quidnunc

[quid-nunk]

A busybody or gossip.

*Columnist Liz Smith
is a famous quidnunc.*

quid pro quo

[kwid-pro-kwo]

This for that. Tit for tat.
An even exchange of one thing for another.

In the chilling thriller The Silence of the Lambs,
*Jody Foster teases information out of the evil
genius Hannibal Lecter by baiting him with his
thirst for knowledge about her personal life, which
she exchanges for information about his crimes,
uttering seductively, "Quid pro quo, Doctor."*

quisling

[quiz-ling]

A traitor.
After the Norwegian politician
Maj. Vidkun Quisling, infamous
for collaborating with the Nazis.

Benedict Arnold was a quisling.

quixotic

[quix-ott-ick]

Rashly romantic.
Foolishly impractical.
From *Don Quixote*, Cervantes's epic novel,
wherein the would-be knight pursues an
outdated code of chivalry, mistaking windmills
for foes and prostitutes for virgin maidens.

*In general, quixotic people
don't do well in business,
whereas Machiavellian people do.*

quod erat demonstrandum (Q.E.D.)

[kwod—air-ot-dem-on-strond-um]

Something that is demonstrated.

In the filmed version of Kazuo Ishiguro's novel
The Remains of the Day, *one of the English
noblemen questions the butler about foreign policy
in an effort to show that the lower classes should be
denied the vote, since they have no capacity for or
knowledge of politics.
When he has succeeded by his questions in
showing that the butler is indeed ignorant
of politics, he says to his companions,
"Q.E.D"—thus it is demonstrated.*

radical chic

Coined by the essayist and novelist Tom Wolfe
in his satirical book of the same name.
It lampoons the mindset of wealthy white
liberals like Leonard Bernstein, who threw
a party for the Black Panthers in his opulent
Park Avenue duplex not, Wolfe implies,
simply because he supported their cause, but
because radicalism was fashionable in the 1960s.

raison d'être

[raise-on-det-rah]

Reason for being.
The be-all and end-all of your existence.
The thing that is most important to you,
or defines you.

Cooking is Julia Child's raison d'être.

rapprochement

[ra-prosh-mahn]

To reapproach.
A peace making or reestablishment of
good relations between two or more parties.

*After the IRA's violation of the cease-fire,
a rapprochement with Great Britain
was thought impossible.*

Rasputin

Grigory Yfimovich (1871–1916).
Eastern Orthodox mystic and holy man.
He exercised undue influence over
Czar Nicholas II and his wife, Alexandra,
because they believed that he could
ease their son's hemophilia.
His abuse of power and notorious debauchery
led to his murder by a group of nobles who,
when poison had no effect on him, shot him
and dumped him in the Neva River.
A Rasputin is someone who exerts undue and
nefarious influence by manipulation,
or someone who just won't die.

realpolitik

A policy of expansion that has as its goal
the advancement of national interest.
In general it refers to a kind of single-minded
and tough political style.

*The outspoken radical feminist writer and activist
Andrea Dworkin has a writing style and a political
agenda that might be called feminist realpolitik.*

recherché

[ruh-share-shay]

Choice. Exquisite. Exotic. Precious.

*The late fashion designer Gianni Versace's
creations were always recherché.*

recto/verso

[wreck-toe/verse-oh]

Front and back.
Right and left.

The right-hand page of a book,
usually with an odd number, is the recto.
If you turn the page and look at the left-hand,
even-numbered page,
you're looking at the verso.

red diaper baby

A child of Marxist parents.

In his recent memoir, Radical Son, *David Horowitz tells his story of being the quintessential red diaper baby, or child of avid members of the American Communist Party, who were determined to raise their children in the Marxist faith, as it were.*

Red Diaper Baby

red herring

A false clue, meant to deceive or distract.
In the seventeenth century, criminals fleeing
from the law found that they could throw
the bloodhounds off the scent by dragging
a piece of cured, strong-smelling
red herring across their trails.
Agatha Christie often used this device
to lead would-be sleuths astray.
It has come to mean anything that
is irrelevant to the question at hand
and intended to distract.

*The drug problem is a red herring
in policy debates over economic problems.*

reductio ad absurdum

[ree-duck-tee-oh-add-ub-sur-dum]

Reduction to absurdity.
A technique in formal logic.
In common parlance it has come to mean
the reduction of part of an argument to
absurdity as a way of denying that
the larger point is valid.

A Modest Proposal *by Jonathan Swift*
was a reductio ad absurdum
on the Irish Question.

revanche

[ruh-vonsh]

To avenge.
Retaliation. Revenge.
A political policy of attempting
to regain lost territory or standing.
Classically used to describe the
politics of Alsace-Lorraine.

*From the German side, the revanchist campaign
was to reclaim the "lost territory" from France,
and from the French side to reclaim
"lost territory" from Germany.*

ring of Gyges

A legend told in Plato's *Republic* to illustrate
that the just life is worth living.
Gyges found a ring that made its wearer
invisible, enabling him to do evil with
impunity. Socrates, however, goes on to
argue convincingly that virtue is its
own reward, and that the just life
is preferable to the life of Gyges.

rive gauche

[reeve-goh-shh]

Left bank.
Refers to the south bank
of the river Seine in Paris.
The bohemian neighborhoods, including
the Latin Quarter, where poets, painters,
and artists of all types make their homes.
Has come to mean stylish in a trendy
or in a pretentious way,
depending on who is speaking.

*The designer Yves Saint-Laurent has a
collection called rive gauche,
which is more affordable than his couture line.*

roman à clef

[row-mon-a-clay]

Novel with a key.
A novel in which the characters are
modeled after real people, and true events
are presented as fiction.

*The recent best-selling political novel about
President Clinton and his campaign, entitled*
Primary Colors, *is a roman à clef.*

salad days

From Shakespeare's *Anthony and Cleopatra*,
it refers to lost youth or naiveté.
Speaking wistfully about herself, Cleopatra says:

*"My salad days,
When I was green in judgment."*

sang-froid

[sang-fwah]

Cold blood.
A certain courageous, fearlessness. Stoic calm.

O.J. Simpson demonstrated a disconcerting sang-froid during his criminal trial for the murders of Nicole Brown and Ron Goldman.

"May I have a bottle of Schadenfreude 1972
or perhaps a Sang-Froid '63?"

savoir-faire

[sa-vwa-fare]

To know how to do.
Knowing how to do things.
An innate or learned ability to know
the appropriate response to any situation,
whether a contretemps or a donnybrook.

Schadenfreude

[shod-un-froy-duh]

Joy in someone else's misfortune.

*Most writers can't help feeling Schadenfreude
when a competitor receives a scathing review.
"It is not enough to be seen to succeed—
others must be seen to fail."—Gore Vidal*

seraphim

[ser-ra-fim]

The highest order of angels.

cherubim

[chair-uh-bim]

The second order of angels.
Cherubim or putti are the pink-cheeked,
pudgy babies with wings who inhabit
the Sistine ceiling.

If someone is seraphic, he's perfect;
if he's cherubic, he's ruddy and plump
with ringlets of golden curls.

shibboleth

[shib-o-leth]

Password, slogan, or byword that is secret
or particular to a certain group.

*The shibboleth of the modern AIDS action group
called ACT-UP is "Silence equals death."*

sic

[sick]

Thus.
In a text it indicates that what came
before was accurate or faithful to an
original text or meaning,
despite the fact that it seems like a mistake.
You see it most often when a scholar
quotes from an original document
in which there is a misspelling.
They want you to know they can spell,
but the other guy can't.
Sometimes it can be a way of emphasizing
the absurdity of what it follows,
as if to say, "Can you believe it?"

*As the irritated mother said to her
hyperactive child,*
"I have just two words for you: Be have!" [sic].

simpatico

[sim-pat-ee-co]

Things or people that are complementary
or a good match.
If you get along very well with someone,
and you understand each other inside out,
you are simpatico.

In The Odd Couple, *Felix and Oscar
were not simpatico.*

sine qua non

[sin-ah-kwa-non]

Not without which.
The essential part without which
the rest is meaningless.

Tartness is the sine qua non of a good key lime pie.

slough of despond

[slaow-of-des-pond]

A state of extreme depression or despondency.
From John Bunyan's allegory, *The Pilgrims
Progress*, in which a Christian falls into a deep
bog on his way from the City of Destruction,
and is rescued by Help.

*Prozac is designed to pull chronic
depressives out of the slough of despond.*

snob

Parvenu. Arriviste.
One who makes a show of social status
of which he is not rightly deserving.
When French monarchs found the need to
refinance the ancien régime they sold titles to
wealthy members of the bourgeoisie.

To silence the outcry of the hereditary nobility,
who were chagrined by the swelling of their
ranks by the unworthy, it was decreed
that all who purchased their nobility indicate
this by adding "sans noblesse" (without nobility)
abbreviated as s. nob. to the ends of their names.

Gore Vidal calls the snobs of
Europe the Perhapsburgs.

soi-disant

[swa-dees-awn]

So-called. Self-styled.

Extremely baggy trousers are all the rage among the soi-disant homeboys.

soigné[e]

[swan-yay]

Sophisticated. Elegant. Fashionable.

The fabulous Miller sisters, who have married a Getty, a Hapsburg, and a prince of Greece, are soigné.

sotto voce

[soh-toe-vo-chay]

Spoken softly. Whispered.
Gently expressed.

*In a library everyone is expected
to speak sotto voce.*

soupçon

[soup-sohn]

A very small amount.
A dash of something,
  often salt or spice.

*Pumpkin bread calls for
a soupçon of allspice.*

sprezzatura

[spret-sa-tour-uh]

Coined by Baldassare Castiglione in *The Courtier*, the essential Renaissance guide to being a gentleman, it expresses the essential quality of such a creature: the unfaltering ability to make even the most difficult things appear effortless, horseback riding through lovemaking.

James Bond is the modern personification of gadget-clad sprezzatura.

stalking-horse

A political candidate used to
conceal the candidacy of a more
important figure, or to draw votes
from and cause the defeat
of the opposition.

*Ross Perot served as a stalking-horse in
the 1992 Presidential election, because
he drew votes away from George Bush,
and thereby helped secure
Bill Clinton's victory.*

straw man

Something that can be easily knocked down.
Like a scarecrow, it looks real, but isn't.
Used in philosophy to describe an argument that
seems substantive but is actually weak.
Usually an argument that no sensible person
would make.

*If you pretend to argue that the world is flat
simply to show how absurd that idea is,
you are setting up a straw man so that
you can easily refute it and bolster your
real belief that the world is round.*

Straw Man

Sturm und Drang

[stirm-un-drang]

Storm and stress.
The title of a 1776 play by
Friedrich Maximilian von Klinger.

*When Othello found the handkerchief
his relationship with Desdemona became filled
with Sturm und Drang.*

succès d'estime

[suck-say-day-steam]

A critical success.
Something that is praised by the critics.

Van Gogh's Starry Night *was not a
succès d'estime in his lifetime.*

sui generis

[soo-ee-gen-er-is]

Of its own kind, unique.
There's nothing else like it.
They broke the mold
when they made that one.

The Artist Formerly Known as Prince
is sui generis.
So was Liberace.

sword of Damocles

Frustrated by the laments of an
envious friend, King Damocles gave up his
throne for a day to demonstrate the
considerable burdens of ruling.
When the friend noticed that an enormous
sword was precariously suspended by
a single hair over the throne,
he quickly gave up the chance to rule.
In this way Damocles brilliantly expressed
the full weight and constant threat
that come with the wielding of
power and high privilege.

Sword of Damocles

tabula rasa

[tab-u-la-ra-za]

Erased tablet.
Philosopher John Locke's term for
the blank slate of the human mind before
it is filled with experience.
Anything that has been erased
and made new again.

*After a serious head injury and a
prolonged coma, your mind might be a
virtual tabula rasa when you awake.*

terra firma

[tare-uh-firm-uh]

Solid ground.
Dry land.

The angry young man found certainty,
the terra firma he longed for,
in the teachings of the Communist Party.

terra incognita

[tare-uh-in-cog-neat-uh]

Unknown territory.

Years later on his deathbed, however,
he found himself questioning his beliefs as
he felt himself slipping into terra incognita.

tête-à-tête

[tet-a-tet]

Head to head.
An intimate, private conversation.

Though neither spoke a word of the other's language, Reagan liked to boast of his tête-à-têtes with Gorbachev.

thánatos

[than-a-toss]

Death.
Often opposed to eros,
which is Greek for romantic love.

*Sigmund Freud posited eros and thánatos
as two of the principal driving forces
in human nature.*

time's arrow

Unlike space, time has a direction;
cause and effect only work in one direction.

In his novel Time's Arrow,
*Martin Amis made a play on this
expression by beginning the book
with the end of the plot,
forcing you to read the story backward.*

Time's Arrow

tour de force

[tour-duh-force]

An exceptional achievement or great work.
Usually of art.

Shakespeare's Hamlet,
*Laurence Olivier's performance
in* The Entertainer.

to wit

That is to say.
Namely.

*March twenty-first is the vernal equinox,
to wit, the beginning of spring.*

troika

[troy-ka]

A Russian sleigh drawn by three horses.
Any group or alliance of three.

Stalin, Churchill, Roosevelt.
Huey, Luey, Dewey.

trompe l'oeil

[tromp-loy]

To deceive the eye.
An effect in the decorative arts
that makes one thing appear like another.
Wood is painted to look like marble.
A flat ceiling is done up to resemble a dome.
An interior room is decorated as an arbor.

Trompe l'oeil is the artistic equivalent of fool's gold.
It looks like what it isn't.

triptych

[trip-tick]

A painting on three panels.
Commonly used to describe anything
in three parts.

O hallowed triptych of the Western world:
money, beauty, youth.

Übermensch

[oo-burr-menshh]

Superman.
The philosopher Friedrich Nietzsche's
term for the man who existed above the
common people of no consequence,
or the rabble.

*Nietzsche considered the composer
Richard Wagner the archetypal
Übermensch, or the closest thing thereto.*

veni, vidi, vici

I came, I saw, I conquered.
The conquering ancient Roman's view
of the world as expressed by Julius Caesar.

videlicet (viz.)

[vee-duh-lee-sit]

That is. Namely. To wit.
Used to introduce examples or lists.

*September twenty-third is the autumnal equinox,
viz., the beginning of fall.*

voir dire

[vwar-dear]

To see say.
To tell the truth.

*When lawyers are selecting a jury for a
trial, they ask questions of all prospective
jurors as a way of determining whether
they can be fair and unbiased
in a particular case.
The process is called voir dire.*

volte-face

[volt-fahs]

An about-face.
A complete reversal. A turnabout.

*The bombing of Pearl Harbor precipitated
a volte-face in America's commitment to
neutrality in World War II.*

vox populi

[vocks-pop-you-le]

Voice of the people.
Popular opinion.

*Though it was highly censored,
Radio Moscow purported to be the
Soviet vox populi.*

Waterloo

Decisive and final defeat.
The Belgian town where on June 18, 1815,
the British army under Wellington
defeated Napoleon.

Watergate was Nixon's Waterloo.
Iran Contra was Oliver North's.

Wergild

[veer-gild]

Man gold.
Blood money.
Old English term for money paid in
compensation to the family of the murdered.
A legal process initiated in the
Middle Ages as an alternative to the bloody
history of vengeful feuding.

To some, in his memoirs,
former Secretary of Defense Robert McNamara
tried to pay Wergild for the Vietnam War.

Weisenheimer

[vise-en-hime-er]

A wisecracker.

*Radio personality Howard Stern
is a Weisenheimer.*

Weltanschauung

[velt-un-showw-ung]

Worldview.
Welt, world, and anschauung, view.
Ideology.
Philosophy of life.

*For all who survived, the Holocaust
forever altered their Weltanschauung.*

Weltschmerz

[velt-schmertz]

World pain.
World weariness.

*His mordant wit was the sign
of his chronic Weltschmerz.*

Whig and Tory

Two parties in British politics.
Whigs can be compared to radicals.
In English history they favored a reduction
of royal authority and an increase in
parliamentary power.
Tories can be compared to modern conservatives,
they emphasized order and stability and
traditionally supported the power of the crown.

will to power

The passion to rule.
A simultaneous act of creation and war.
The new "good" or highest standard of life.
In his book *Thus Spake Zarathustra*,
Friedrich Nietzsche introduced this concept
as the most fundamental in his philosophy.
He considered it the greatest power on
earth and the secret to life.

*The Cambodian dictator Pol Pot
was a slave to his will to power.*

Wunderkind

[vun-der-kind]

Prodigy.
A talented youngster.

Mozart was a Wunderkind.

Zeitgeist

[zite-guyst]

The spirit of the times.
In *Phenomenology of Spirit*, the philosopher
Hegel posited a spirit of the world that was
embodied in each era by a different person or
movement and passed down through the ages.
The spirit of each age is called the Zeitgeist.

*The Zeitgeist of our times is embodied by
cyberspace and fat-free food.*

ABOUT THE AUTHORS

Norah Vincent
is a staff writer for the *NY Press*. She holds a Bachelor of Arts in Philosophy from Williams College. Her writing has also appeared in *The New Republic* and *The Weekly Standard.*

Chad Conway
is an editor at The Free Press, Simon & Schuster. He holds a Master of Arts in European Intellectual History from McGill University.